Finding Freedom

A Basic Guide to Forgiveness and Reconciliation

Bill Irwin

© Copyright 2014   William M. Irwin
Oak Tree Ministries
www.oaktreeministries.net

All rights reserved. This book is protected by the copyright laws of the United States of America. This book may not be copied or reprinted for commercial gain or profit, or in substantial or entire form for personal use or distribution. The use of short quotations or occasional page copying for personal or group study is permitted and encouraged.

ISBN: 0692243607
ISBN-13: 978-0692243602

Unless otherwise noted, Scripture quotations are from The Holy Bible, English Standard Version® (ESV®), copyright © 2001 by Crossway, a publishing ministry of Good News Publishers. Used by permission. All rights reserved.

Verses marked NASB are taken from the NEW AMERICAN STANDARD BIBLE®, Copyright © 1960, 1962, 1963, 1968, 1971, 1972, 1973, 1975, 1977, 1995 by The Lockman Foundation. Used by permission.

DEDICATION

I thank God for all those who have sat with me and taught me through the years of my journey. Some have been there to help me; some have come to me for help. All have taught me!

I am especially grateful for my wife and life-partner, Beth, and her continued love and grace. In all our years together, she's consistently lived a life dedicated to following Jesus and seeking the greater things He told us we would do (John 14:12.) I learn from her every day! I am a blessed man.

CONTENTS

	Preface	vii
	Introduction	ix
1	A Short Story	1
2	Forgiving	5
3	Reconciling	25
4	A Little Longer Story	49
	Appendix: Helpful Resources	61

PREFACE

There are many, many books and articles out there about the power of forgiveness. Right now looking across the room at a single shelf on a bookcase in my office I can see books and materials by Neil Anderson, Charles Stanley, Leanne Payne, John and Paula Sandford, Alfred Ells, and James Friesen that all are dedicated to healing past wounds, and either all or in part cover forgiveness. And there are so many other resources. Some are older, some very recent.

So why another book?

I don't pretend that I have any different answers. The people mentioned above have great insights. So do many others.

I do have a different voice, though, and it's my prayer that my voice can help one more person along the road to the freedom Jesus purchased for us on the Cross. I learned years ago that sometimes all a student needs is a different teacher to finally "get it." I pray that this short book will help you on your journey where others have not.

I've also been very concerned over my years in ministry about the confusion I often see between forgiving and reconciling. In my view, they are intimately tied together, but they are different. Separating the two has been powerfully helpful for many in ministry sessions. Again, I pray that this book will help you along your journey.

The book has been kept short for a reason ... it's my goal for the reader to be able to work through it in an hour or so, to end with understanding forgiveness and reconciliation, to be able to put both in place in his or her life, and to have hope that God can and will bring freedom as he or she follows His ways of dealing with past wounds and broken relationships.

May God bless you as you read. "And I am sure of this, that he who began a good work in you will bring it to completion at the day of Jesus Christ." (Philippians 1:6)

INTRODUCTION

When someone wounds us, we have choices to make. We need to choose what to do about the negative feelings and thoughts that flood through us. And we need to choose what to do with the fractured relationship. The first decision involves forgiving. The second involves reconciling.

Over the next several pages we'll look at both forgiveness and reconciliation.

There's something vital to understand at the beginning ... *forgiveness and reconciliation are not the same thing.* We'll explain more in depth as we go, but ... *forgiveness is about dealing with God and the wound as an individual; reconciliation is about rebuilding the relationship around trust for each other.*

We often get the two confused, and that causes the whole process to break down.

(And if you're afraid I'm going to tell you that you have to reconcile in an unsafe relationship, that's not going to happen. In fact we'll see that Jesus actually tells us there are times not to pursue being in relationship with an offender. I'll explain more as we go, but be at rest ... you won't be sent back into danger.)

We find Jesus' major teaching about these two things in Matthew 18:15-35. He starts with reconciliation and moves on to teach about forgiving.

To help us understand this whole passage a little better, and why Jesus approached the ideas of reconciling and forgiving this way, we need to also understand that the Jews and their rabbis in Jesus' day usually taught from the ending and ultimate point to the beginning points. We do the opposite. We start at the beginning and build our case to the main point.

Think of it this way ... Jesus would say, "Here's the whole house, I want you to see it in it's finished state. And now that you've seen that, here's where we started." We much more tend to say, "Here's where we'll start, and then here's what it will look like when it's all done." He starts with the conclusion and goes back to show the points along the way. We tend to teach by building point by point until we reach the conclusion.

Jesus taught first about the end process, reconciliation, in Matthew 18:15-17, and then moves on to teach about the foundation of forgiveness in Matthew 18:21-35. And in His teaching the middle section, verses 18-20 become a hinge upon which both depend.

We're going to look at all this the way we usually do, and deal with forgiveness first and reconciliation second. We'll start at the end of the passage, look for a bit at the middle, and then cover the beginning.

And a final note as we begin ... as I tell stories I've changed names and some details to protect the identities of the individuals involved. All the stories are based on real life situations.

Matthew 18:15-35

15 "If your brother sins against you, go and tell him his fault, between you and him alone. If he listens to you, you have

gained your brother. 16 But if he does not listen, take one or two others along with you, that every charge may be established by the evidence of two or three witnesses. 17 If he refuses to listen to them, tell it to the church. And if he refuses to listen even to the church, let him be to you as a Gentile and a tax collector. 18 Truly, I say to you, whatever you bind on earth shall be bound in heaven, and whatever you loose on earth shall be loosed in heaven. 19 Again I say to you, if two of you agree on earth about anything they ask, it will be done for them by my Father in heaven. 20 For where two or three are gathered in my name, there am I among them."

21 Then Peter came up and said to him, "Lord, how often will my brother sin against me, and I forgive him? As many as seven times?" 22 Jesus said to him, "I do not say to you seven times, but seventy-seven times.

23"Therefore the kingdom of heaven may be compared to a king who wished to settle accounts with his servants. 24 When he began to settle, one was brought to him who owed him ten thousand talents. 25 And since he could not pay, his master ordered him to be sold, with his wife and children and all that he had, and payment to be made. 26 So the servant fell on his knees, imploring him, 'Have patience with me, and I will pay you everything.' 27 And out of pity for him, the master of that servant released him and forgave him the debt. 28 But when that same servant went out, he found one of his fellow servants who owed him a hundred denarii, and seizing him, he began to choke him, saying, 'Pay what you owe.' 29 So his fellow servant fell down and pleaded with him, 'Have patience with me, and I will pay you.' 30 He refused and went and put him in prison until he should pay the debt. 31 When his fellow servants saw what had taken place, they were greatly distressed, and they went and reported to their master all that had taken place. 32 Then his master summoned him and said to him, 'You wicked servant! I forgave you all that debt because you pleaded with me. 33 And should not you have had mercy on your fellow servant, as I had mercy on you?' 34 And in anger his master delivered him to the jailers, until he should pay all his debt. 35 So also my heavenly Father will do to every one of you, if you do not forgive your brother from your heart."

1 A SHORT STORY

John and Lisa asked to meet with me several years ago. They'd been married about eight years, and had three small kids. Lisa had grown up going to church and John had come to faith a little before they got married. The first few years had been a bit rough but they had seemed to be doing well the last couple of years. And they loved each other. A lot! But now they couldn't stop fighting with each other. Both carried pretty strong personalities. Peaceful days rarely happened in their home any more.

I'd walked with them before through some hard issues, but now they questioned if they could stay together. As we talked neither could really identify why they were so unhappy with each other ... they just couldn't seem to see eye to eye about anything. They did love each other, and they loved their three children, but neither one could see going on in a marriage like this.

I hadn't known Lisa well when they got married, and didn't know John at all then. The church was large and I hadn't been involved with the wedding. It's easy to hide in a large setting. I just remembered being surprised when I first heard the news. Some things spilled out in their story as I asked some questions.

Early in their dating they became physically intimate, and Lisa soon became pregnant. Only her parents knew. The decision to marry had been made quickly ... it turned out they hadn't been married at the church but had gone to a 24-hour wedding chapel a few hours away and had the ceremony performed there. They'd returned home, lived with her parents, and managed to hide the details in the large setting of the church.

Listening to them a few things came through loud and clear ... shame, disappointment, anger, distrust. They'd talked some about the shame, mostly to keep it covered over. But not the disappointment. And definitely not the anger and the distrust.

Both had been very willing participants in the premarital sex. But neither had dealt with their feelings about all that happened ... a baby when they really weren't ready ... having to grow up too fast ... and the distrust of knowing that they had caused some major problems for one another.

Lisa felt justified in her anger. John hadn't protected her. He knew she was a believer, and she didn't believe that having sex before marriage was ok, but ... well, things happened and it felt really good and she enjoyed the attention. She felt guilty the first time, and told him. She felt guilty the next time, too. And the next. But they continued. She freely admitted that she wasn't pressured. But he didn't protect her by stopping. And then the baby came. And a marriage too soon. She never felt she could trust him to protect her.

John was angry too. Lisa had let him know she was a believer, but she didn't act like it. She never had said "no" as intimacy progressed. And she actually often initiated the hugging and kissing and physical contact. He knew she was feeling guilty and he was puzzled by that, and wondered why she never called a halt to things. He never had the upbringing she did and thought she would help him do the right things.

And then the baby came. And a marriage too soon. He never felt he could trust her to stand up for the things she said she believed.

Both of them felt cheated of their last growing up years, pressured to be adults and grown up when they weren't ready. Both were disappointed in themselves and in each other. Life had been hard. They kept trying to make things work between them without acknowledging the hurt and anger they carried. And now it wasn't working.

Talking together a little more, they both realized they had been trying to be in their marriage when they never had admitted that they were hurt and angry about not being able to trust each other. They would look across the room at one another with the thought at the bottom of their hearts ... "I know what you did to me and I don't trust you."

They forgave each other in my office that afternoon. Each asked and gave forgiveness. Each owned their part. Lisa forgave John for not protecting her and keeping her safe. John forgave Lisa for not living up to her beliefs. They forgave each other for the hardships they had caused one another. They forgave each other for the pressure they put themselves in. They forgave each other for the secrecy. They forgave each other for the distrust they had allowed to fester. Tears flowed freely that afternoon, and we joked about needing to take out stock in a tissue company. At the end all the tension left the relationship.

I continued to talk with them over the next months, and the fighting never started up again. A few things had to be reworked in their relationship, almost starting again from the beginning. They began enjoying one another and a whole new level of love. It's a happy home because they took the steps first to forgive and then by working on trust to reconcile.

2 Forgiving

Every building needs a foundation. Every relationship does, too. Forgiveness is a major part of every relationship and its foundation.

Unresolved wounds in relationships keep causing more wounds and damage the foundation of the relationship. Forgiveness deals with those wounds.

We understand this very well in our physical bodies. If for some reason you've been cut by broken glass and you realize some of the glass is left in the wound, you get that broken glass out of you! If it's small and easily seen, you maybe can do it yourself. If it's hard to see you get help, maybe even going to the emergency room at the hospital to have an expert remove the glass. You clean the wound, care for it, and do what you can to promote healing.

Our spirits and souls, our hearts, are not really different! I'm amazed at what we tolerate in our hearts that we'd never allow in our bodies! Why should we allow the thing lodged in our heart that wounded us and keeps wounding us to stay?

Forgiveness accomplishes the removal of the "thing" that caused the wound and that keeps hurting us. Like broken glass, it may have just one sharp edge, or it may have several. It still needs to come out and the wound needs cleansing and care. Our hearts can be made whole again.

Ministry leaders, physicians and researchers all have observed a number of emotional and physical costs to unforgiveness. Emotions include anger, stress, anxiety and depression. Physically, there's high blood pressure, stroke, heart disease, poor immunity to diseases, and even cancers that thrive in an atmosphere of bitterness. We don't have to live with those things!

We don't forgive because the other person deserves it ... we forgive because we deserve the peace that comes with wholeness.

Jesus gives us all the keys in Matthew 18:21- 35.

Who's Responsible?

The passage starts when Peter asks Jesus a great question about forgiveness. "Jesus, my brother keeps sinning against me. How often do I forgive? How much do I forgive?" (See Matthew 18:21-22.)

Look carefully at what Peter says ... "How often do *I* forgive my brother when he sins against me?" He understood this key thing ... *forgiveness is about us, not the person who injured us.* It's about what we're feeling, about our heart, not the person who hurt us. It's not about the other person asking for forgiveness. It's really not about them at all. It's all about us. It's about what we're thinking and feeling. Peter is taking appropriate responsibility for what is going on in his own heart.

Peter's question and Jesus' answer help separate the differences between forgiveness and reconciliation. It's our thoughts and feelings about the whole thing that Jesus addresses with forgiveness. What the other person does or does not do about the situation affects reconciling. (And if the person is not coming to us to make things right, it's one more thing to forgive!) It's a two-step process: forgive first, then work on reconciling.

Honestly, we usually really want the other person, the offender, to come to us and apologize (or even grovel a bit ... groveling helps!) We often wait for that to happen (and usually it's a long, long time!) "They did it ... they should come to me first. I shouldn't have to go to them." And when they don't come and apologize, our anger grows. And grows.

Partly what's happened is that we have gotten our responsibility and the offender's responsibility mixed up. While it is always the offender's responsibility to make the necessary steps to repair the relationship (reconciling), *it's always our responsibility to deal with our feelings and thoughts about the offense and the offender.*

Waiting for the offender's remorse surrenders our responsibility for our own feelings and our own thoughts. We give the offender more power ... and it's our power. We become dependent on their choices and allow them to determine how we feel and what we think. It's not a great trade-off!

Forgiveness is about dealing with all the reactions down inside of us; reconciling is about dealing with the relationship. Forgiveness is about one person ... "me." Reconciliation is about two people ... "we."

So ... we take responsibility for our own reactions by stepping into forgiveness.

Let's face it ... when we're hurt, we're hurt. When we're frustrated, we're frustrated. When we're afraid, we're afraid. And when we're angry, we're angry. It doesn't ever do any good for us to sugar coat it and pretend that everything is fine with us as we try to deal with a tough relationship issue. Down inside we know that we're still dealing with all the negative feelings toward the other person.

Forgiveness starts with being honest with ourselves and with God about what is going on down inside of us.

What About Revenge?

Peter's question also opens something up for us that helps us understand when forgiveness is complete. He asks Jesus, "If my brother keeps sinning against me, how long do I have to keep forgiving him? Seven times?" He's being honest here, and actually generous.

The rabbis of Jesus' day taught that we were obligated to forgive three times, but after that we could do whatever we wanted. The rabbis allowed for us to "get even." We could nurse the wound and let it spill out. We could get justice.

Most of the time we want justice ... or more. We want to get even. We want the other person to feel the full measure of the pain we have felt. We want to retaliate. We want revenge.

Peter offered generous terms ... "Should I double what the rabbis teach and add one more time to be safe?" But ... he was asking, "How much do I put up with before I take matters into my own hands and get even? When can I let my anger out?"

Jesus responded with a number that made it clear ... we can't go there. How often do I forgive? How much do I forgive? Every time. Every thing. The number Jesus gave (seventy-seven times, or seventy times seven, depending on the translation you use) purposely was big. He was saying, "Peter, you can't keep count. Retaliation isn't an option in forgiveness."

Peter's question leads to this ... if we harbor thoughts of hurting the other person somehow, or making them pay for what they've done, we have not truly forgiven.

Yes, we may still be hurting and what has happened may still be very painful for us, but we don't have to react with a desire for revenge.

(And please understand, there may be legal consequences for the other person, or consequences from other sources, such as an employer. Our giving testimony or participating in a legal solution does not mean that we have not forgiven. Setting appropriate boundaries and creating safe distance between us and the other person if they don't make full efforts of reconciliation is not unforgiveness. Forgiveness is simply about our own heart attitude.)

In our hurt, we may have fleeting thoughts of revenge, *but fleeting thoughts are not the same as harbored thoughts.* Satan and his workers excel at throwing negatives and lies at us hoping they will stick. We can't always keep that from happening, but we can choose to let Jesus have control. We can choose not to dwell on the negatives. Martin Luther has been credited with saying centuries ago, "you can't prevent the birds of the air from flying over your head, but you can keep them from making a nest in your hair." Satan loves to tell you that you haven't forgiven just because a quick thought of revenge runs through your mind. That's not true. When it comes, tell the thought and the spirit behind it to leave.

Part of the reason for the "seventy times seven" comes from the tactic Satan and his workers continue to use. Your enemy will continue to prompt those thoughts of retaliation and revenge. It will continue to prompt thoughts of how much you were hurt. Keep resisting them. Keep telling them to go. Don't quit just because they keep coming! They *will* stop

Jesus told Peter he couldn't *keep* the thought of revenge and retaliation tucked away to be pulled out later. He couldn't give it room to grow in his mind and heart. He couldn't allow it to stay. Then Jesus explained why.

Kingdom Priorities

God operates His Kingdom primarily out of mercy.

Jesus told Peter a story, the parable of the unforgiving servant (Matthew 18:23-34.) A king decided to settle the accounts of his servants. He called in a man who owed him millions of dollars, and found the man couldn't pay. At first the king was going to have him and his family sold but the man begged for mercy. The king decided to be merciful, forgave the debt (wiped it clean) and sent him on his way.

The servant, though, came across a fellow servant who owed him what amounted to lunch money. Instead of doing what the king had done so graciously and letting go of the debt that was owed him, he physically attacked his fellow servant, refused to listen to his pleas for mercy and had him thrown in prison.

The rest of the king's servants were appalled. They knew everything that had just occurred. They went to the king and told him what had happened. The king called the first servant back in and asked why he had not done as he had done. The king denounced his wickedness and threw the unforgiving servant into prison. Literally, the words Jesus used were "... he gave him to the torturers to be tortured."

Then Jesus says this is what Father God will do with those who don't forgive.

And please note something here ... the king didn't take back his original forgiveness of the first servant. In verse 32 he says, "I forgave you all that debt because you pleaded with me." He nowhere says he's reinstating the debts. Verse 33 makes it clear the king is angry because the servant didn't extend mercy to his fellow servant. That is why he was left to the devices of the tormentors.

We forgive because we have been forgiven. We show mercy because we have been given mercy.

We have been forgiven of much, and we forgive others the same way. God forgave us of all we have done to cause separation between Him and us ... Jesus died a horrific death on the Cross to make that possible. He expects us to turn loose of our anger and hurt and forgive those who have wronged us.

As God forgives us He never ever has told us that our sins are "okay." Our sins are not transformed into something that's somehow excusable or even good. They are what they are ... sin ... wrong. He's just said He will forgive us and not hold them against us any more.

What was done to you was not okay then, and it is not okay today. It will never be okay. It was wrong then and it is still wrong. Forgiving what was done does not transform it into something that's okay. It remains what it is, a sin and a wrong. But it does not have to stand between us and peace. Forgiving allows us to put aside the pain and hurt from what happened and come to a place of peace in our own hearts.

The person who hurt us is still responsible before God for what they have done.

It's Past

There's another way to understand this ... what has been taken from us is still gone. In Jesus's story, all the money taken by the first servant from the master was still gone. It wasn't going to come back. The amount misused and stolen was so big there was no way the servant could repay. The master was bearing the cost of the servant's sin against him.

What the master did by forgiving was refuse to let the wrongdoing cost him any more. The money was gone, but he could keep his peace by forgiving the debt. He chose to put an end to his own turmoil over what he had lost; he would not lose any more or pay any more for what the servant had done.

By forgiving the debt of the servant the master made a decision to give up hours and days of worrying, keeping track of what payments were or weren't coming in, watching over the servant's further actions ... He chose to let the servant off his hook, and to *let himself off the hook.*

Understand this: what you've lost in this relationship is already gone. You've already paid the price of the loss. Forgiving now lets you move on beyond what you've lost ... it doesn't have to dominate your thoughts, your emotions, your life from here on out.

And ... what happened is in the past. What is hurting you now are the thoughts and emotions of today. The past will not change. It won't somehow become better! We have to give up the thought that our past will somehow become better. We've mentioned before that what was done to us was wrong then and it's still wrong. We can't change that! We can only choose God's way and live beyond that.

Refusing to forgive is like continuing to make payments on something that has already been paid for. I love a good bargain, and paying extra is never a bargain. Why do it?

No, forgiveness is not "fair." But why keep on paying for the wrong that was done? Why open ourselves to continual torment?

Our power is in precisely the letting go of the offense, just as God did with us. It's the power to move into peace and to move away from the offense and the offender occupying so much of our thoughts and emotions.

How Big?

There's another twist in this story ... "big" and "little." Millions of dollars and lunch money.

For many of us the temptation to make excuses for little things is huge! "Oh, it's not that big a deal." But we seethe inside. A paper cut may not cause a lot of blood loss, but it still bleeds a little and it still hurts! We'll get a Band-Aid and not worry about it any more. But add up a hundred or so paper cuts and we might as well have been stabbed with a sword.

A few years ago I met with a friend, a ministry leader in our area. Bob seemed frazzled and restless. I asked him what was going on, and he told me that he had been working a lot of extra hours. I asked about any time off, and he mentioned that he had finally gotten a few hours off the day before and had really been looking forward to it. He'd gone for a hike to spend some time enjoying a beautiful spring day, but got a call from his wife letting him know that another couple wanted to meet with him about something they said was urgent for the ministry. They had told his wife it was absolutely necessary, and the only time they could meet was just two hours from then. They were going to meet at his home.

Bob turned around on his hike and walked as quickly as he could to get back to his car, rushed to get home and cleaned up. The beauty of the day was quickly left behind as he pushed himself to get home. He reached his front door about fifteen minutes before the couple was due and ran in, quickly showered and came out on time.

They didn't show up.

An hour or so later, Bob called, and they told him, "Oh, we decided it wasn't that important after all. We don't need to meet with you." By now it was the time he had originally set to start home, and the rest of the day's schedule was waiting for him. Too late to hike any more, he started on some paperwork until his next meeting.

I asked him simply, "Have you forgiven them?" Surprised, Bob looked across the room at me and said, "I didn't know I needed to."

"Did it bother you?"

"Yes."

"Did it inconvenience you?"

"Yes."

"Did they take something away from you?"

"I hadn't thought of it that way, but yes."

"What did you feel when they didn't show up, and then when they said they didn't need to meet you after all?"

"I was really frustrated and it's been hard still to settle down."

We talked a few more minutes and prayed together, and I led him to tell God he forgave them for being so inconsiderate of his time, and of actually robbing him of his only time off in weeks. Bob described a huge weight coming off him, and he began relaxing right there in front of me. He was at peace.

It doesn't matter if it's a big offense or a little one ... We need to forgive!

Torment

If we don't forgive, we are left to *"... the torturers ..."* (Matthew 18:34, NASB.) It can be fully translated *"... the torturers to be tortured ..."* or *"... the tormentors to be tormented ..."*

If we don't forgive, our problem is not God's unwillingness to take away our hurt and pain. Our problem is our decision to let Satan and his workers continue to torment us. Instead of protecting ourselves we leave ourselves open to continual pain and torment.

The Apostle Paul told the Ephesians in his letter (4:26-27) to go ahead and get angry but not to sin. Then he said to deal with it before the sun went down, and not give Satan a place or a foothold or an opportunity. The Greek word he used for "place" is <u>topon</u> (the root for our word "topography") and it means a physical place. Anger that is not worked through gives Satan a location in our lives from which he can work

Satan and his workers will nurse your hurt into anger. Anger untended can grow into bitterness. Bitterness becomes rage. Rage unchecked blossoms into hatred. And at every turn the thoughts and ideas of injustice grow. You dwell on how terrible the offender is and how you have been victimized. You have difficulty getting those things off your mind for any length of time. It's hard to be happy and joyful, and that usually fades quickly back into the negatives. It can be all consuming.

Jesus said, "The thief comes only to steal and kill and destroy. I came that they may have life and have it abundantly." (John 10:10) Satan is there to steal the life Jesus intends for you, to kill you and destroy all that is rightfully yours.

It's not my purpose in this little book to go into the depth of the spiritual warfare involved, but please understand, *the war you feel inside has its roots in unforgiveness, and Satan wants you to stay in turmoil.* Paul says further in Ephesians 6:12 ... "For we do not wrestle against flesh and blood, but against the rulers, against the authorities, against the cosmic powers over this present darkness, against the spiritual forces of evil in the heavenly places."

Satan loves telling us a lie about forgiveness ... that forgiving means giving up our power and safety. That is not true.

Torment, and the tormentor, goes away when we forgive. What was done to you is still not excused and somehow made okay, but you take away its ability to hurt you even more. And you take away the enemy's right to torment you. Your power is precisely in your ability to let the offense go and forgive the offender.

Even if the offender never steps up and makes things right, you will still be free. Just like Jesus paid the cost of our sins, we pay the cost of the other's sin. But ... we gain freedom and peace, and we don't have to demand that they repay us. And Satan doesn't have the place any more to continue to accuse and torment us.

Is forgiveness hard? Yes. The cost can be high. Humanly it may be impossible. But with God all things are possible.

Binding and Loosing

Let's cycle back a bit to Matthew 18:18, and then verses 19-20.

Jesus said in verse 18 that whatever we bind on earth is bound in Heaven.

Matthew's Gospel was written in Aramaic, the Hebrew dialect of Jesus' day. Anyone hearing those words from Jesus in Israel, or reading them later as someone who understood Aramaic, would grasp the easy, common meaning of the expression. Rabbis of the day used the language often. To "bind" something meant simply to forbid it. To "loose" something meant to allow it.

Context in scripture is one of the keys to understanding it. Jesus said these things about binding and loosing in the midst of teaching about reconciling and forgiving in relationships (Matthew 18:15-35.) The words here are more about relationships than spiritual warfare ... the same words in Matthew 16:19 have much more to do with understanding our role in spiritual battle.

There's a powerful key here ... *What needs to happen is not natural, but supernatural.*

If we bind forgiveness here and don't allow it, it's bound and not allowed in Heaven. We literally prevent God from working. It's like we've taken a package and hugged it so tightly to ourselves that no one else can take it out of our hands. We may beg and plead with God to take away our pain and torment but we prevent Him from helping us by refusing to forgive. We prevent Him from doing the very thing we want Him to do (and the very thing *He* wants to do.)

And if we've bound God from working in the offense, we've also bound Him from working in the offender. We don't allow it. We may have been asking Him to get ahold of the other person's heart, but we've bound Him. No matter how much we've prayed and asked God to work in the offender we actually keep Him from doing it.

Loosing our pain, though, allowing forgiveness, gives all the weight and glory of Heaven room to operate. God can work in our hearts no matter how big the offense. And God can work in the offender's heart.

One of the roots behind the word forgiveness is to cut a knot in cords that have tied something up. Jesus says we can bind things ... keep them tied up ... or we can loose them and get them totally untied. We can sever the knot that has kept us tied to our pain. It's not just cutting the cord. That could leave enough for us to tie ends together and bind things up again. But if we cut the knot we just leave small pieces, not enough to tie it all together again. We are free to let God work and bring us His freedom.

Then in verses 19-20 Jesus promises that the Father will do for us what we ask, and He promises us He will stand with us. "Again I say to you, if two of you agree on earth about anything they ask, it will be done for them by my Father in heaven. For where two or three are gathered in my name, there am I among them."

These words have often been taken out of context to apply to power in numbers for prayer purposes. (You know ... "Will you agree in prayer with me about this?") That point is not wrong, but it's not the main point. Jesus is teaching about relationships here.

We desperately need God's help to forgive! God's promised help is not a wish, but it's active. He *will* and *does* help.

Have you noticed in many of the miracles of healing that Jesus performed He asked the person to do the very thing that was impossible to do? "Stretch out your hand." "Rise up and walk." He knew they couldn't. But He also knew that He was there with them, and the power of God was there to accomplish the miracle. All He really was asking of them was to start the process ... "Tell your arm, your legs, to move." When they began to obey His words, the healing came.

The same thing happens in forgiveness. We begin doing what He tells us to do, and He makes it happen. We start saying the words, "I forgive," and he finishes the work. We're no longer bound and no longer tormented.

People often tell me "I can't forgive." That's why we need His help! And that's why He gives us His help! All he asks is that we start.

We have to be careful that "I can't" really isn't an "I won't." Please don't buy the lies of Satan and his workers! Decide to set yourself free. Decide to take all the help that Heaven can give. You *always* have a choice.

You may be saying right now, "But you don't understand what the other person did to me. You don't understand how horrible it was. You don't know the damage it caused. You don't know how much I've suffered." You're right. I don't.

But God does.

He saw it all and He understands it all. He's promised to stand with you and to bring all the power of Heaven to help you.

He also sees and understands everything you have done and thought and believed that kept you separated from Him, and He sent Jesus to die for you to bring you back into fellowship with Him, literally to give you new life.

The greatest injustice in the world fell on Jesus, fully God and fully Man, without sin or fault. He took on Himself the punishment that brings us peace (Isaiah 53:5.) In the Cross is the peace you so much desire.

God is not being unfair. He knows what has happened to you, and He is asking you to let go of the pain, the fear, the hurt and the anger so you can have His peace.

He has paid the price of the Highest Treasure of Heaven to forgive you. He is asking you to forgive whoever has hurt you.

How to Make Forgiveness Happen

The following steps can be done at one time and will provide the spiritual basis for you to be released and live in God's peace. It may be helpful to have a trusted friend with you to help you as you walk through these steps. You will find a very rapid release!

These steps are acts of the will. Your emotions will follow! If you're struggling to start, ask God to make you willing. "Lord, I'm willing to be made willing" is a legitimate and powerful prayer. Then step into the process.

1. Be honest with yourself and with God about what you are feeling and what was done to you. Spell out the details.
2. Get the details outside of you. Tell them to God. It's best

to speak them out loud. If needed, write them out (but don't keep re-reading it!)
3. Make the statement out loud to God to forgive. Be definite (not, "I hope to forgive," or "I want to forgive.) Name the offender and tell God what they did and what the results have been in your life. Be thorough ... don't rush through this, but also don't dwell here. Just start, and God will help you through the words.

It's most helpful to say, *"I forgive _____ for _____ and I release him/her to You, God. I take him/her off my hook and put him/her on Yours. I release all my rights to judge _____, and I leave judgment to You, God."*

4. State the following ... *"I renounce the lie that I have to live in unforgiveness, anger and pain. I break all agreements I have made with unforgiveness, anger and pain. I declare that God gives me His peace, and I choose to live in forgiveness and peace."*

5. Finally, send the spirit of unforgiveness away. Make the following declaration ... *"In the name of Jesus and by His power and authority, I send the spirit of unforgiveness away from me. I send it to Jesus, and it has to go where He sends it. It cannot return, and it cannot send another like itself."*

For most this will be enough and will bring powerful and rapid release. It's important to understand that spiritually, *it is enough.* It's finished in the spiritual realm.

Where some run into problems is in picking up the offenses again when old feelings start to intrude. Your emotions may take time to completely recede. *But if you have taken the steps to forgive, it's done in the spiritual realm.* Remind your emotions of that. And remind Satan and his tormentors of that. "At this place and at this time I forgave."

Keep reminding them as long as it takes to be at perfect peace. If need be, keep going back to the statement above in step 4. Be patient and walk it out ... you *will* come to a place of total peace.

Satan will tell you that because you "feel bad" you haven't forgiven. Not true! Renounce it as a lie, step into the truth that you have already forgiven and move ahead.

Again, it will be helpful to do this out loud. When we're verbalizing something out loud, our mind fixes on those words. We literally are telling ourselves what to think!

It's crucial to bring your mind back to thinking about the fact that you have forgiven. Our emotions always follow the "facts" we dwell on. Brain scientists have shown repeatedly that the right side of the brain, the emotional side, responds to the scene being considered in the left side, the fact side. The right side thinks it is happening "right now." Telling yourself and reminding yourself that you have taken the steps to forgive moves that "fact" from the left side to the right side, and your emotions will respond positively.

Scripture speaks in a handful of places about this process with our minds ... "Finally, brothers, whatever is true, whatever is honorable, whatever is just, whatever is pure, whatever is lovely, whatever is commendable, if there is any excellence, if there is anything worthy of praise, think about these things. What you have learned and received and heard and seen in me—practice these things, and the God of peace will be with you." (Philippians 4:8, 9 ESV) .... "You keep him in perfect peace whose mind is stayed on you, because he trusts in you." (Isaiah 26:3 ESV)

Stay patient as you walk it out. Remind yourself that you have forgiven! God has promised you peace and He will give it to you.

3 RECONCILING

Because we've already done the work of forgiving the other person we can enter the process of reconciling from a position of strength. We've let the hurt go. We aren't demanding anything from the offender, aren't demanding that they repay us for the hurt they've caused. We aren't even more vulnerable to being hurt. Instead we can give them a chance to rebuild our trust, to rebuild the relationship and to do it voluntarily.

God provides safety for both of us in His way of doing things. Our forgiveness creates an atmosphere of safety for the offender to repent and to make things right. And reconciliation gives us a place of safety, even if it means saying to the offender, "I see you don't really value me or our relationship, so I'm free to not give you my full trust any more." We can have an appropriate level of trust, or if needed we can exclude them from our lives.

We all know what it's like to have someone approach us with anger. Not fun! We get defensive pretty quickly. More likely than not, we'll respond to the *emotion* rather than the *content* of what they're saying. Walls go up and listening stops. We likely can't even get to the content of their message to deal with the reasons behind the emotion.

That happens when we approach the offender with anger, too. The interaction is almost doomed from the start.

This doesn't mean we have to wait until we have no feelings about what's happened! In fact, our feelings are a big part of what needs to be addressed. What happened *is* a big deal! We've been hurt, injured, and the offender needs to know that. But ... *our anger coming from the hurt is our issue, not theirs. That's why we forgive first.*

Forgiving and doing that hard work first gives reconciliation a chance. Forgiving first gives us a chance to begin confronting what has happened between us with hope it will change.

Confrontation at its very best becomes an invitation to the other person to change. It's an invitation to move from what has been to what can be. It moves the past into the present and makes room for something new in the future.

Jesus laid out the process in Matthew 18:15-17. Go to them and tell them what they've done that has caused the problem. (And remember His other instructions ... the other person may be having a problem with *you* and it needs to be worked out ... Matthew 5:23-24. And James 1:19-20 adds instructions about being quick to listen, slow to speak, and slow to anger.). The attempt is to get you both to a place where the relationship is restored. Going alone preserves confidentiality and prevents unneeded embarrassment if the person repents. It will help, too, if you can give them an idea of what they need to do to start making things right. (In a few more pages we'll look at what to do if this means facing someone who is dangerous ... for now work this through.)

If they don't respond to you, Jesus says next to take a few witnesses ... get help from a few others. This protects both of you from being abused further. It protects you from words being misunderstood and later misquoted, and it protects the offender from you making unreasonable demands.

If that doesn't work, He says "tell it to the church." Simply today, widen the field of those who know the situation and get more help, ideally from spiritual leadership.

And if getting more help doesn't work, put them on the outside of those you trust.

I've purposely abbreviated the explanation of these steps, but they're crucial. Go. Go again with help. Go a third time with more help. Stop going.

Reconciliation, which Jesus is teaching about in these few verses, is simply about rebuilding trust. It's *not* about saying you're sorry and playing nice. I remember hearing those words a fair amount when I was growing up ... and it never worked. One or both of us involved would still be angry, and something would blow up again later. We didn't trust one another after a forced "Sorry!"

And trust ... trust is about safety and respect. When we know we will be safe, when we know we will be respected, trust flourishes. Without either of those it's hard for us to trust.

It's helpful to think of relationships and trust levels like a target on a piece of paper. You know the kind ... a spot in the middle that's the bull's-eye, and then all the rings around it that get wider as you move out from the center. The people you trust most belong in the center. For most of us it's a fairly small group, maybe two to four or five people. They know everything about us, and they love us and protect us. The next ring out are good friends ... they know a lot, but not everything. By the time we get to the outside ring we're dealing with people who we don't know at all ... they're strangers. The rings in the middle we trust more, the ones further out we trust less.

Jesus tells us to move through this process of reconciling by keeping the person who hurt us in the appropriate circle on the target. One who belongs in the bulls eye or the next circle can stay there if they make things right. And one who was in the bull's eye or the next circle has to be moved to the outside of the target if they refuse to take the steps to reconcile and rebuild trust.

The game plan Jesus gives really doesn't change at any step He outlines. We're to tell the other person what they've done and what we need to be able to trust them. That's true if we're there by ourselves, or have taken another with us or have gone with even more support. The purpose at each of those steps is always to try to return to a place of mutual trust. Tell them what they've done and give them a chance to start making it right. And depending on their response we keep them closer in the circle of trust or we put them on the outside.

In all this, I often see one of two things when reconciliation is needed. Some people never make the attempts to work through the relationship issues and wind up with a string of broken and failed friendships and loves. If they offend someone, they don't make the effort to clear things up. If they're hurt and they make any attempt at all, it's to punish. They don't forgive, and they don't try to reconcile. They choose torment and distrust over the possibility of safety and respect. They miss the chance to see God at work when the other person is willing to work on things. They choose to bury and carry pain. They've forgotten or ignored the first part of Jesus' teaching ... "Go tell them..."

And some never stop pursuing the ones who won't make things right. They continue to run after them and leave themselves open to be hurt over and over. They choose to continue being made unsafe and disrespected when it's clear the other is not trustworthy. They miss the chance for God's peace to reign in their lives even though the other person is unwilling to work on things. They choose ongoing and renewed pain over peace. They've forgotten the last part of Jesus' teaching here ... "Treat the offender as an outsider."

Let me say it again ... being in relationship with another person is about trust ... trust that there is mutual caring about the relationship ... trust that there is mutual respect ... trust that we're safe together ... trust that both value the relationship enough to do what it takes to make it work.

What About Punishment? And Control?

It's vital to understand that reconciliation is not about punishing the offender. Punishment is not mentioned anywhere in these verses. There's a wonderful question that explains why in Romans 2:4 (NASB) ... "Or do you think lightly of the riches of His kindness and tolerance and patience, not knowing that the kindness of God leads you to repentance?" *It's the kindness of God that leads us to repentance!* It's not His punishment! Repentance comes from being loved. Reconciliation happens when it's approached from a position of love for the offender.

Trying to punish the offender with the hopes of repairing the relationship never works. It only leads to emotional pressure and resentment for both people. Punishment leads to fear. ("There is no fear in love, for perfect love casts out fear. For fear has to do with punishment, and whoever fears has not been perfected in love." 1 John 4:18) The offender needs to be able to trust us, too, if reconciliation is going to happen.

Fear in us can drive us to the desire to control, and it's that desire that leads us to want to punish. And the fear comes from having been hurt before. Punishment says "I have to be sure you're never going to hurt me again, so I'm going to control you by causing you pain."

It's easy to get into a cycle ... we're afraid ... we try to control ... we get hurt ... we're afraid of more pain ... we try to control again ... we get hurt again.

Reconciliation can happen when we decide to get off the merry-go-round of that cycle. We really never can control another person, but we can *influence* them.

Remember, reconciling is based on trust. If we feel we need to control the other person, we really simply don't trust them! That means we have already determined they don't belong in a close circle of trust ... they need to be on the outside.

Telling the offender what they can do to help rebuild trust *is* a good thing. It's not punishment to ask someone to go to counseling or a twelve-step program. It's not punishment to say you need to have something they broke or ruined replaced. They may not like hearing those things, but the requests are a path toward building trust and restoring the relationship. Give them a chance to respond.

Trust thrives on love. It cannot survive in fear.

The effort to truly reconcile by the one hurt says, "I want to let you know what has happened and give you a chance to make it right. I want to trust you again." It's not accusation (even though it states what's wrong.) It's not demanding punishment. Those things create another cycle of offenses going the other way. It *is* giving the offender a chance to make things right. At its best it's an invitation to renew and deepen the relationship.

Rebuilding Trust

The effort to truly reconcile by an offender says, "I value you and our relationship more than what it costs me to make things right between us. I want you to be able to trust me again." We're looking for an attitude; a heartfelt desire to heal the hurt and a determination to do whatever it takes to make that happen.

Anything less indicates the offender is not to be fully trusted.

Look at it this way ... if I've caused a problem for you or damaged you in some way, you question whether I care about you. When you make me aware of it, if I don't do something to demonstrate that I care, I've shown that I'm not trustworthy. It's my job to try to make things right and regain your trust.

Say I've borrowed your car with a promise to return it that same evening by 6:00 PM. The time comes and goes ... it's 6:30, then 7:00, then 7:30. You call, and I tell you, "I'm sorry, but I was in an accident right after I borrowed your car. It looks pretty bad. I sure hope you've got good insurance." Our friendship is probably totally gone, and you definitely are not going to trust me after that.

Or let's say we've got the same situation ... borrowed car and an accident ... but this time I call you to break the news. "I'm sorry I wrecked your car. It's been towed to a repair shop, and my insurance is already working to get it repaired. Oh, and there's a small amount available for you to get a rental car. You'll have to go down there to pick it up." You make arrangements to get the rental car, and find all they have for you for the time your car is being repaired is a used car full of dents, different colored body panels and 4 bald tires. Plus you don't know the quality of the repair shop, and what kind of parts they're going to use to make the repairs. The accident and repairs could affect the resale value of your car. It's all a hassle. But I've made sure my insurance is going to get your car fixed. At this point, you and I may still have some kind of friendship, but you're not very likely to let me borrow anything valuable again.

Or ... same situation ... I call and tell you this ... "I've got your car at the best repair shop in the area. They're making it a priority, and I'm making sure they're using all factory parts. I've called the car rental agency, and they're sending someone over to get you. When you get there, I want you to pick whatever rental car you want for as long as it takes. I'll pay any extra costs at the rental agency for you to have what you want. Oh, and I'm arranging for another shop to install the best sound system your car will take in it." You're feeling pretty good about my efforts to make things right at this point. Then the day comes to get your car back. It's in great shape, the sound system is beyond wonderful, and you find a $500 gift certificate to a nearby place for you to get the music you want for your new system.

By now you're just waiting for me to ask to borrow something again!

God laid out this principle in the Old Testament laws about restitution. You can read some of that in Exodus 22, or again in Leviticus 5:5-7. His purpose was simply to make the statement, "This is what's right when you've caused financial damage to another. Do what it takes to make the other person whole again, and show them you value the relationship."

In reconciling, the offender makes the one who was hurt and their wellbeing the focus. It's not about excuses. It's not about "getting out of trouble." It's not about "I'm really sorry." *It is about "I've hurt you and I want to make it right. I want you to be ok again."*

For reconciliation, the offender has the responsibility to make the needed repairs to the relationship. The offender has the task of rebuilding trust.

So, go and let the offender know what they've done ... give them a chance and watch their response ... get help if you need it ... if they don't make it right create appropriate distance between you.

Going Sideways

As you take the step to confront the offender, it's crucial that you be clear about what you need for the relationship to be restored. If you just need them to own up to what has been done, that's fine. If you need them to take other steps, that's fine too. But you need to have a good idea of what it's going to take before you go.

I watch many attempts at reconciliation go sideways because the one starting the process doesn't know where they want it to go and what they want the offender to do in response. The requests change, and the offender watches the restoration target move at every new turn. Usually this comes from the one hurt not having done the forgiveness work first.

This is a good place to get help from someone who can give you wise counsel. The more you know about what you want the easier the process will be.

The process can also go sideways when the offender offers something else than what has been proposed. Remember what we just said in the last section? The offender has the task of rebuilding trust. And ... the one who was hurt determines what that needs to be.

If they're proposing a better solution, it will work. But if they're proposing something that is simply more convenient for them, or easier for them to do, what does that communicate? "I don't want to do what it's going to take to make you whole. I don't value you enough to put in the effort."

If you're the one who has been hurt, be clear what you need and don't settle for something that doesn't show you are valued.

Another way this can happen is by the offender agreeing to something and then trying to find a way around it.

Jeri came to me one evening to talk about problems that she was having with her mom. Jeri's grandfather molested her when she was in early grade school. She told her mom, and her mom denied anything had happened in spite of the physical evidence right in front of her. Her mom even helped her clean up and got rid of the torn and soiled clothes, but she still denied anything had gone on. She told Jeri not to say anything to anyone about it. Jeri obeyed her mom, and also managed to stay out of situations where the same thing could happen again.

As an adult, she got up the courage to confront her mom about her earlier denial. Mom held her ground, but they still maintained a relationship. She forgave her mom for not dealing with the situation and did the best she could with that wall between them.

But now Jeri's daughter was about the same age she had been, and she couldn't live with the idea that her mom might not keep her little girl safe ... her mom had to own up to what had happened for her to feel safe leaving her daughter with her.

We talked about her previous attempts, and she decided to try one more time with a letter detailing out what had happened to her, the evidence she knew her mom had seen, and the need for her mom to acknowledge what had happened. She wrote the letter, included a time by which she wanted a response, and sent it off.

I remember clearly asking her, "Are you prepared for her to deny it again?" She thought for a moment.

"Yes. I know it may not work. But I've decided I'm going to have to cut her out of my life until I know my daughter will be safe."

The time for her mom to respond came and went, and Jeri asked me to come sit with her while she called her mom to tell her what was going to happen.

"Mom, I know you got my letter, right?" Her mom said she had.

"Mom, I don't want you to contact me or my husband or my daughter again until you're ready to talk to me first and clear up what happened all those years ago with Grandpa. I mean it. No contact. You can call me when you're ready to admit what happened, and we'll go from there."

She hung up the phone, and we talked and prayed a bit more, and I left. She hated what was going on, but she was at peace.

About a month later Jeri called again and asked me to come over. The postman had dropped off a large package, addressed to her daughter. It came while her daughter was home, and she'd seen it. She was excited because it was her birthday in a few days, and she knew the package was for her and it was from her grandma.

"Jeri, what do you think your mom is trying to do?" She got more upset the more she thought.

"She's trying to avoid it all again, and she's going around me to get to my daughter."

"What are you going to do?"

Jeri called her daughter in ... "Honey, I know you're excited about the package, but we can't keep it. Grandma wasn't supposed to send it." Fortunately her daughter didn't ask why, but she still was getting upset.

Jeri did something brilliant then. She grabbed her purse and pulled out a twenty-dollar bill and gave it to her daughter and told her, "We're going to the post office to drop this package off, and then we're going to the toy store. You can get anything you want with the money I just gave you." She chose to pay the cost so her daughter wouldn't miss out.

A few days later Jeri's mom called. "Why did you send the package back?"

"I told you, Mom, no contact with any of us until you're ready to talk to me."

Her mom started to deny that Jeri had ever told her that. Jeri said simply, "Mom, my pastor was here when I called you about the letter and told you that you couldn't contact us again. He knows exactly what has happened and he knows what I said to you."

Her mom hung up on her.

The birthday went by. Another week or so passed. Jeri's mom called. "Can we talk?"

Jeri made arrangements, and they sat down the next day and finally began to work things through. It turned out her mom had been molested, too, and it had been such a painful memory she just didn't want to deal with it. When Jeri first told her mom all those years ago her mom had begun to relive her own painful history. By getting everything out in the open, Jeri and her mom were finally able to have an honest relationship.

Consistency

Another way reconciling can go sideways is in the area of consistency.

I mentioned above the "moving target" that can get set up by someone who has been hurt that makes it nearly impossible for the offender to do what's needed to help the relationship heal. That's one way consistency is critical.

It's critical for the offender to be consistent in their efforts to restore things, too. Consistency builds trust and creates safety. It says, "You can count on me to do what's best for you."

Mark and Tonya came to me from first working with another pastor through the initial aftermath of Tonya finding that Mark had repeatedly been unfaithful to her.

She made the discovery when an emergency came up with one of their children. Mark worked a good distance away ... an hour's drive with no traffic, but of course there was always traffic. He'd told her several times that he wasn't allowed to take personal calls at work. He told her his bosses had made it clear that personal calls were grounds for termination, so she never questioned when her calls to his cell phone went unanswered. He was just working late. And of course that's what he told her every time. *But this time it was critical that she reach him.*

Tonya called Mark's cell, hoping he'd pick up the call. She tried a few more times. When he didn't pick up she scrambled to find the phone number for the company he'd written down for her a few years before just in case something like this happened. When she got the switchboard, she asked to be connected to him and she was told that he'd left the office hours earlier. She explained her emergency and asked for someone to go check to be sure he wasn't there somewhere.

The individual on the switchboard sent a security officer to look for Mark and stayed on the phone with Tonya because her panic was very, very clear. After awhile, they said, "I'm sorry, but he's not here. His parking spot is empty, and he clocked out when I thought he had. I'm so sorry."

Things began to unravel that night as she demanded to know where he was earlier. At first, he lied and tried to slough it off. Over the next few days Tonya gathered more information and found out it was normal for Mark to leave mid-afternoon. He usually wasn't home until very late at night.

She insisted they meet with the other pastor, and the whole story came out. There had been several women, usually ones he met at bars. When he wasn't with another woman, he was at a bar ... he'd drink some early and then stay until enough alcohol had left his system for him to drive home safely.

Her shock and anger at the betrayal was understandable. Surprisingly, she was willing to try to work things out ... and so was Mark. He legitimately regretted what he had done and he wanted to change. We worked together for a number of weeks, sometimes the three of us together, sometimes just her, sometimes just him. They worked hard.

One of the biggest sticking points was that Mark had never really been accountable to anyone for his time. There were a few meetings he had to be at for work every week, but his schedule was generally somewhat flexible. Most in the office kept fairly set hours, so Mark agreed to do that and he gave Tonya the go ahead to call his office to see when he arrived and when he left. He got her the phone numbers for everyone from his bosses to the janitor at the building. And he agreed to answer his cell phone when she called. He called her every morning when he arrived at work, and he called again to let he know when he was leaving. And he agreed to call if something was delaying him getting home at the expected time, and he'd give her an updated arrival time.

Things were working well.

Then I noticed him beginning to lose some of his initial desire to make the relationship work. I talked to him a bit about it. He admitted he was getting tired of making calls every time he had a change in his schedule. We talked again about the need to rebuild trust. Tonya was coming around, and things were better, but I could still see in her some anxiety about Mark every time we met.

The Holy Spirit began to talk me about their situation. I shared with Mark.

"Mark, checking in with Tonya every day is crucial. She has been so hurt it's going to be a long while before she fully can trust you again."

"How long?" he asked.

"Three years. You can write it in your calendar. It's going to take three years for her to fully trust you again. The clock started the day you started letting her know everything."

"You're kidding!" He began to get a little angry.

"Mark, she's not punishing you. She just needs to know you are going to be where you say you will be. She needs to be able to trust your word. There were so many lies and evasions it's going to take time. She loves you, Mark, or we wouldn't be this far along."

He calmed down. "I know. I hurt her really badly."

"Mark, there's one more thing. The first time you're late ... more than 15 minutes late ... the clock is going to reset to day one. It will be another three years. You need to call. If your cell phone stops working you need to get off the road and find a phone somewhere."

"You're kidding! Right?" He was getting upset again.

"No, Mark. I'm not kidding. She was hurt that deeply. You can go two years and eleven months and be late, and it's going to reset the clock. For some people it's a different time, but that's what it's going to take."

He thought a moment. "Okay. I understand."

The Spirit kept talking to me ... "Mark, you won't get another reset if that happens. You're only going to get one chance."

He looked at me and nodded. We prayed together and he left my office.

The call I was hoping wouldn't ever come did come nearly two years later. He'd stopped somewhere on the way home to look at some computer things for their house and had bought them. He had the goods and the receipts with the time on them. But he hadn't called. Tonya's anxiety had blown up into a full panic attack within a half hour after he was supposed to be home. He drove in about an hour late to find her frantic, shaking all over and screaming at him, throwing all his clothes out of their room

They came in the next day, and he did what he could to make things right. In her head she knew what had happened, and she tried to put it behind her. But it was evident a new time clock had started. She wasn't at a place yet where he could test her trust. As we talked, he asked her forgiveness for letting her down, and they committed to continue together to try to make things work.

They had a few other road bumps along the next three years, and Tonya especially struggled as they started again. Mark stayed patient and repaired the damage he'd done. From beginning to end of the process it took them over five years. But they made it. They're moving ahead with a good marriage and a great family.

Dangerous People

As we finish looking at verses 15-17, we need to address something else. Though Jesus says we have the responsibility to go to the offender when we've been hurt or wounded, I want to make it very clear that I do not believe He is sending anyone back into a situation where they are likely to be abused again or where there is a threat of harm or violence.

No victim of a molestation should be told to go back alone to confront the molester. No victim of rape should be told to confront the rapist alone. No victims of abuse or violence should be placed alone with the aggressor.

The victim's words, "stop it," or "no," or "leave me alone" ... even their tears ... are communicating to the offender that they're causing harm and the victim is suffering. Clearly to me, the first step of telling the offender what they've done *has happened through those tears and those pleas to stop.* There's no need for the victim to go back again into a situation where they can be traumatized again.

It's not even a good idea for the victim to be made to confront the aggressor even with others present. The only appropriate responses here are for others to go as advocates for the victim, or to initiate and follow through with legal help. Any helper brought into a harmful situation has the primary responsibility of keeping safety, especially for the victim, as a primary goal. (Keep in mind that while the Old Testament examples given above talk about restitution for a loss, we're talking here about actions that the Old Testament says would cause the offender to be excluded from the community of Israel, or even put to death.)

Confrontation does not work when it comes from a position of weakness or a place of fear. It has to come from a position of strength, not from a place where the victim can be hurt again.

In confronting, we have to be prepared for the very real possibility that the offender will not respond well. In that light, forcing a victim to face someone dangerous simply victimizes them again.

Remember, we're dealing with an incredibly fragile trust. Any trust that was there for the offender has been broken in the worst ways. If the offender was a stranger, there was no basis for trust there to begin with except maybe a child's basic trust for adults. That has been shattered, too. Forcing anyone who is a victim to place himself or herself in danger again will only cause more fear and totally erode trust in those who are "helping!" Remember what Jesus said about fragile, young hearts ... "Whoever causes one of these little ones who believe to stumble, it would be better for him if, with a heavy millstone hung around his neck, he had been cast into the sea." (Mark 9:42 NASB)

Binding and Loosing; Continuing and Stopping

Jesus' statement in the next verse, Matthew 18:18, takes us further into reconciliation. He says "... Whatever you bind on earth is bound in heaven, and whatever you loose on earth is loosed in heaven."

Two things stand out about reconciling here (and remember what we shared in the section on forgiveness.)

First, we have the power to "bind" or forbid a behavior in a relationship, and we have the power to "loose" or allow it. And if we do that here on earth, it has the same effect spiritually. In more common terms of today, we have the ability to set the boundaries of our relationships. And keep in mind this applies to the verses before.

More than just ability, Jesus gives us a mandate. He requires us to set the boundaries of our relationships. Whether individually, or as advocates in a tough situation, or as churches, we can forbid or permit behaviors (and of course that includes attitudes.)

Another way to say it ... *we set the atmosphere of our relationships.* Jesus asks us to establish the atmosphere of our homes, our family relationships, work relationships, church relationships, our neighborhoods, our cities ... our world.

There's a story from my parent's marriage that illustrates this. Dad grew up in a very difficult, poor and violent home in the dust-bowl era of Kansas. He and his brothers and sisters did not have the security of knowing whether they would eat in a given day, or if they would be living in the same place the next week, or if they would be subjected to a violent, alcohol fueled outburst by my grandfather. Mom grew up in a more stable environment in the same era ... her family owned a dairy. They always had food and they had a decent home. Life for her wasn't perfect, but her parents were loving and kind.

My dad was a good man, but he carried some of his childhood scars into their marriage in 1940. The story is that he got upset with my mom one day, and reached out and slapped her. When he started to do it one more time, she grabbed his hand, stopped him and told him, "If you ever do that again I'm leaving." Dad never raised a hand to her after that.

Mom "bound" that behavior, and heaven protected that decision. She also "loosed" an atmosphere of love and safety and respect, and heaven promoted that.

Second, we have the ability to forbid or permit a relationship to continue. Going back a bit, that's the clear message of verse 17 ... if an offender won't listen to the church, treat them as an outsider. There's a point to stop the relationship.

There comes a time in hurtful relationships to stop pursuing the other person. Jesus said it's a time to place them on the outside of our circle of trust.

Treating someone as an outsider doesn't mean being angry or bitter or unkind. It just means that we treat someone like a person we can't trust. We can still be kind and courteous while we also put distance between us. Even like we treat people around us in stores and in public places with basic respect we can do the same with those from whom we have had to back away.

Of course, if they continue to be destructive to whatever relationship we have left, we may need to cut the relationship completely off. If you're feeling run-over and disrespected, create the needed distance. Pursuing the offender when they have made it clear they are going to continue their attitudes and behavior keeps the problems going. It guarantees more pain!

When to Stop

So how do we know for sure we've reached the point of needing to treat the offender like an outsider?

Jesus gave the first guideline in verses 15-17 ... is the offender listening to the complaint? This doesn't mean just hearing the words. Nor does it mean simply apologizing and saying "Sorry." Are they doing something to try to make the offense right? Are they working to provide trust in the relationship? Remember, what you're looking for is that they show you they value the relationship and showing that they value you.

Please keep in mind that this might not happen on the spot. Many of us have a hard time when we're confronted fully dealing with everything that is brought to us, and we may not have a clear idea what to do to make things right. As you approach the offender, tell them what they have done, but also tell them what they can do to make things right. And give them a chance to step up to the plate.

It may not happen perfectly, and it may not happen exactly the way you want at first. Remember you're not there to punish, but to help restore. Watch their attitudes. Watch their hearts. If it's important to you it will be important to them.

The second guideline is what we just looked at in verse 18 ... what are the boundaries of our relationship? What do we permit and what do we forbid? What is the atmosphere we expect and enforce with heaven's help?

The final guideline comes in verses 19-20. Jesus looks here at what happens when we come together before God on behalf of our relationships. He promises to work on our behalf to accomplish what we ask, and He promises to stand with us.

We shared about this in more depth in the section on forgiveness ... God promises His help and He promises to be with us.

For purposes of knowing when we've reached the cut-off place for a relationship, He tells us the key is our coming to God in agreement ... agreement for the relationship. Are you both approaching God and asking His help to make the relationship whole again? The story I shared about Mark and Tonya a little earlier is a good illustration of this.

Are you both willing to ask God to work on hearts and attitudes and behaviors? That's really the goal of the "listening" Jesus is talking about in the earliest verses of this passage.

Jesus promises some wonderful things in these two verses.

First, if we come to the Father agreeing we want our relationship to work, He'll do it.

We need to understand that much of what needs to happen in relational breakdowns is spiritual. It's supernatural, not natural. We need the help of Heaven! Things that drive selfishness, bad attitudes and harmful behavior have spiritual roots that can only be handled with God's help.

Promises of "I'll change, I'll change!" are empty (and often designed to just take the pressure off for the moment.) Promises of "I want God to change me" are full of hope.

Two people coming to God and asking His help to change the harmful parts of their relationship have the assurance of Heaven that it will happen.

And Jesus promises further that He will stand with us.

You are never alone in your battle for a right relationship. Jesus stands with you. The One who holds the universe together, the galaxies, stars, suns and moons stands with you. The One who endured the worst behavior ever demonstrated by mankind when He went to the Cross stands with you. He knows the worst that humans can do. He experienced betrayal, rejection, humiliation and shame but now lives in total triumph over them all, and He stands with you.

God promises His help and His presence if the two of you will come together and agree prayerfully that you want to make the relationship work.

So three guidelines ... First, are they listening and trying to make things right and rebuilding your trust? ... Second, do they respect the things you permit and the things you forbid? ... Finally, are they agreeing together with you for God's help to make the relationship whole again?

If those things are not happening, the relationship can't be made whole. It's time to stop pursuing it.

Making Reconciliation Possible

I started to title this section "Making Reconciliation Happen." Even that thought sets up an impossibility! I can't *make* reconciliation happen, nor can you. That's part of the fairy tale lie Satan loves telling us. Even though I have my part in my relationships and you have your part in yours, we can't *make* it happen. There's always another person involved.

Giving up that false belief removes ongoing frustration from the enemy's toolkit. You *can* influence what happens, but the other person involved has their part to play, too. You have *influence,* but you don't have control.

Much of what we've been describing over the previous pages is simply giving up the idea that we can control the other person.

Because there is another person involved, the process of reconciling is not easy to put into a series of words to say. But it all can be boiled down to the simple points we've already made...

... tell them and watch their response ... set appropriate boundaries ... seek God's help together.

In telling them and watching their response, remember that you can call on others to help, one or two at first, then spiritual leaders. Watch how the offender responds to what you are saying, and be open to deal with anything you may have done to cause problems in the relationship, too. If they won't respond to you going to them, even with help, put them on the outside of your life.

Set up what's going to help you trust one another ... decide what you will permit and what you won't in your relationship.

Finally, go to God together. If there have been others brought into the process also, include them. Look for a real desire for God's work in each heart and openness to His work.

I want to encourage you with a final story ... God's ways of forgiveness and reconciliation work!

4 A LITTLE LONGER STORY

Cherie and I connected at church through our small group ministry. She and her husband, Ben, became key leaders as the ministry grew. Cherie always carried an open and free heart. People gravitated to her care and her laughter.

At some point we began sharing some background and realized we both had received help from a ministry half way across the country that brought us major healing from childhood issues. It really wasn't a huge ministry, and the connection was just a fun thing.

Cherie called me one afternoon and asked to come in ... and she told me she knew she was going to need a few hours. We arranged to meet the next day.

She began our time together by saying, "I didn't tell you everything about my ministry time with our friends. I held something back from them and I know it's time to deal with it now."

Cherie began telling me about growing up in her home without her dad from the time she was about nine or so. She'd come home one afternoon from playing with friends after school and walked into their home to find a few suitcases packed at the front door. Her dad and mom waited for her, dad in front and mom standing several feet away, quiet and glaring. He knelt down and told her he had to leave, that he loved her and he wanted her to be brave. He never said anything about when he would come back. He held onto her for a few minutes while she cried and then he kissed her on the forehead and walked out the front door, bags in hand. He hadn't said anything else, and her mom hadn't said a thing during the whole time.

Cherie didn't know what to think or what to say. Her mom made it clear she didn't want to talk about it. Cherie cried herself to sleep that night, and the next ... and the next.

She asked her mom again a few times when Dad was coming back, and her mom didn't give any real answers. Days stretched into weeks, then months ... and years.

One more time she asked a question ... "Why doesn't Dad call?" Mom again made it clear she didn't want to talk about it. Cherie never asked again.

Their life before had been predictable and good ... lots of love and laughter. They especially enjoyed church together. Now the household settled into a new life ... Mom, Cherie and her little sister, and Cherie's grandmother moved in, too.

Soon it was junior high, then high school ... dating, dances ... church and a growing faith. And she missed her dad. She missed him a lot.

Her mom didn't know, but Cherie often cried for her dad. Nights were the worst. The house quieted down at bedtime, and she'd lie there remembering that afternoon when her dad walked out the door and out of her life.

Cherie told me about days she would cry for hours, missing her dad and wondering why he had left her. She couldn't figure out what she had done that was so bad that he would leave her and not want to have anything to do with her again.

Until he left, he had usually been the one to take her and her sister to school each morning on his way to work. He'd listen to their sleepy chatter and smile. She missed the rides in his truck and the hug and quick kiss as she got out each morning.

Every new event brought pain again. The first day of school every year ... the first day at junior high ... the first day of high school. Then there were the dances and proms ... and no dad to tell her how pretty she was. No dad to talk to her about how to relate to a boy. Graduation, and no dad to be proud of her.

She moved out of her home to go to a university, and dad was nowhere around. She wondered what he would have said to her ... she cried many times over the first weeks of school ... alone and scared she pushed through.

Cherie met Ben at school and they fell in love. He was a good guy ... at least she thought so. She wondered what her dad would have thought about him. An engagement and wedding plans came soon ... the morning of the wedding dawned with a flood of tears again. Cherie's dad was not there to tell her how beautiful she was, to walk her down the aisle, to give words of wisdom ... he wasn't there to give her away ... instead she felt thrown away.

Children came ... her mom and grandmother shared in her joy as she and Ben grew their little family. And she wondered what could have been and she grieved.

Once he called her. He just said, "Cherie, this is your dad. I wanted to know how you are." She froze when she heard his voice. All the hurt and anger that had grown over the years came flooding up and she didn't know what to say.

"I'm ok."

She told me that he asked another question or two, and that she answered with short, clipped words. After another awkward moment or two, he asked her to write down a phone number, and told her she could reach him there.

And that was it.

Until she called me.

That day in my office as we talked and prayed together, Cherie poured out her pain to God. She literally screamed a few times in anger and in pain. She sobbed and let everything come out. We met for about three hours. She knew enough from her previous ministry time to be thorough. God met her wonderfully and comforted her. As we worked together, we continued to ask Him where He had been, and He showed her ... at every stage He had been there. Even on that awful afternoon when her dad left Jesus had been standing beside her, holding onto her.

Cherie fully forgave her father. And she left my office with no more pain and totally at peace.

A few weeks later Cherie called me again. "I'm going to call my dad tonight. Will you pray with me and pray for me?" We prayed for a few minutes on the phone, and I agreed to be in prayer during the time she had decided to place her call.

They talked for several minutes. Cherie told him that she knew that Jesus wanted her to forgive him for not being in her life all those years, and she could hear him weeping on the other end of the phone. She told him about her husband and her three children. He asked some questions, and told her he had been praying for her over all those years. They both cried a bit more. And they promised to talk again.

She called me the next morning to tell me what had happened. We praised God together and I remember we asked Him to do whatever more He wanted.

Over the next month, they talked again a few times. He asked for pictures of her and her husband and the children.

She got an address and then mailed them off. God was repairing her heart and repairing their relationship bit by bit.

Cherie called me again a month or so later.

"Bill, you're not going to believe this. Ben just called me and he's being transferred. We're being moved into the city where my dad lives. We have to be there in two months."

Only God could do this. Cherie knew it. She knew God was working a miracle.

It wasn't a small move ... the new city was a few thousand miles away. They had to sell their house and pack up a young family with all their belongings and prepare their kids for leaving their friends and the only life they had known so far.

We talked a few times over the next few months, and got together to pray again a day or so before they left. She had called her dad and he knew they were coming. He mentioned the possibility of them getting together. We prayed about that and asked God to orchestrate everything.

Cherie called me again a few weeks after they moved.

"I'm going to go meet my dad for dinner tonight. Ben will be home to take care of the kids, and dad and I are going to meet at a restaurant nearby. Will you pray for me? For us? I'm going to ask him why he left."

We prayed and just asked Jesus to go with her to dinner and do what He wanted. Cherie admitted a few nerves colored her confidence. I asked her to call me when she could and let me know how the meeting had gone.

When she called the next morning, I wasn't ready for all she told me ... she hadn't been ready for what her dad told her the night before.

After they had been together for awhile that night and had finished most of their meal, Cherie asked the "elephant in the room" question...

"Dad, why did you leave us?"

Her dad opened up quickly and carefully ... and with tears streaming down his face.

"Honey, I don't know what happened that day, but when I got home that afternoon your mom was more angry than I had ever seen her. She accused me of having an affair and told me to pack my bags and leave. I tried to ask her what she meant, and she wouldn't let me talk. She was so angry. She screamed at me and threatened me. And she told me that if I didn't leave she would, and she would take you and your sister and I'd never know where you were. And she told me I couldn't contact her or you again, or she'd just disappear. She meant it, honey.

"She was so angry!!! I didn't know what else to do, so I did what she asked."

Cherie's tears started long before her dad finished.

"Dad, why didn't you say something to me?"

"Honey, I told you ... your mom was too mad. I was afraid I'd never see you again. I never did what she said I did. I've never been with anyone else ... ever. Not even in all these years since."

Cherie cried more and then choked out, "I thought you didn't want me any more. I thought you didn't care."

"I know, honey. I heard the hurt in your voice when I called you a few months back. But I've had to be so careful. I was afraid of what your mom would do, and I've been afraid of what you've thought."

What happened next still amazes me. Cherie's dad began telling her what his life had been like over the last years.

"Cherie, you never knew it because I had to hide from your mom. I used to park my truck down the street from your school every day where I could see you and your sister walk by on your way to class after you had been dropped off. When you went to junior high, it got a little hard because you were in different schools, but I'd trade off and go where I could see you one day and then where I could see your sister the next."

She sat with overwhelming emotion surging to the surface. Things she'd never imagined began welling up inside. And of course more tears came.

Her dad continued on ... he'd been outside the school regularly. He sat in his truck down the street when she went to her first prom, hoping he'd get a glimpse of her and her date. On graduation day he'd been outside the gym. He'd watched them drive off the morning she left for college.

On her wedding day, he'd been down the street. He'd watched her and Ben run through the crowd and the thrown flowers and rice to their getaway car, and they'd driven right by him. He described the car to her, described what she'd been wearing. She knew he was telling the truth.

As she wept, she got up and moved to his side of the table and reached her arms around him. And he did the same. They wept together and hugged one another. Cherie told me it seemed like it was just minutes, but when she checked her watch they'd been there for hours.

I was weeping, too, as I listened to her. We praised God together.

And then Cherie said, "I need to talk to my mom."

We prayed some more, thanking God for what He'd already done, and asked Him to go with her to meet her mom.

Cherie called her mom later that day and made arrangements to meet her a few days later. She lived a few hours away, so childcare would be an issue. Ben readily agreed to take time off work to take care of the kids.

At the meeting, Cherie directly told her mom that she had met with her dad and what he had told her. She asked her mom for an honest answer ... "Why did you think dad was having an affair?"

"Your grandmother told me she had been driving by a motel in the end of town where your dad was supposed to be working that day. She told me she saw him coming out of a room along with another woman as she passed by. She was positive it was your dad."

"But he said he never was unfaithful to you. He still hasn't been. You never gave him a chance to defend himself!"

"What he did to me was awful! Your grandmother ... she's my mother! Why would she lie about something like that?"

Cherie understood why her mom had been so hurt, but she still didn't have answers. She called again and we prayed some more. A conversation waited with her grandmother.

Another day went by while Cherie arranged a time to meet. Her grandmother had moved some years ago to another town and Cherie drove a good distance to her place, praying the whole way for truth to come out.

Cherie's grandmother welcomed her and they sat at her kitchen table.

"Grandma, why did you tell Mom that you saw Dad coming out of a motel room with another woman? He swears he's never been unfaithful to Mom ... he still hasn't after all these years."

Cherie watched her grandmother stiffen, her eyes narrowed a bit. "I never did like your father."

And that was it. No other answer.

Cherie sat back, stunned. Tears streamed down her face as she remembered every step she'd taken to be free of the pain she'd carried so long. This woman she thought loved and cared for her and her mom and her sister had destroyed her life with a lie. The betrayal went to her deepest core.

But Cherie had come too far down the road of healing to let things end now. She gathered herself in the midst of her tears and told her grandmother what she had been working through. She could see her words hitting home.

Her grandmother began to sob. Before she could say anything, Cherie walked around the table and held her, and said, "Grandma, I forgive you. I'm not going to let this destroy my life any more. I forgive you."

Cherie told me that her grandmother apologized and acknowledged she had been wrong. There really wasn't a lot more she could do to make things right. Cherie used her grandmother's phone to call her mom and told her what had happened. She told her mom on the phone she forgave her for not digging to find the truth, and then she handed the phone to her grandmother so she and her mom could talk. Her grandmother and her mom began the process of working things out between the two of them.

Cherie drove back to Ben and her children that night. She explained things to Ben ... he held onto her while she talked and he did his own forgiving as the hours stretched deep into the night. She'd been right all those years before when they first met ... he really was a great guy. He'd stood with her through this entire journey, encouraging her and praying with her and for her. And now they were close to the end.

The next morning she called her dad and arranged for him to meet her and Ben for lunch. Ben had never met her dad, but he reached for his hand to shake it when they met, and then pulled him close and told him, "I am so sorry." Those words broke any remaining ice.

Cherie's dad came to their house after lunch and was waiting with them when the children got home from school. They knew Cherie had been talking with their grandfather but they hadn't expected this. It was a little strange to have him there. He stayed for dinner, asked lots of questions and began a new relationship with his family. They warmed to him pretty quickly.

Cherie kept in touch with me as things developed over the next few months and years. She told me that she got to watch her dad become an incredible part of her children's lives. It brought healing to her heart a little more each time she saw him loving his grandchildren, playing with them, helping them with schoolwork, being involved in their lives at every chance. She thanked God often for bringing him back into her life.

Ben and her dad grew into great friends and often did things together. It warmed Cherie's heart!

She called him "Dad" from the beginning, but she realized over time what a treasure he was to her ... a very wise man ... a friend ... someone she trusted completely. He truly became a father to her.

And there's more ... Cherie worked through the issues with her mom before her mom passed away just a few years after all this started. And she worked to repair the relationship with her grandmother.

Another few years went by, and I got another call ... "Bill, my grandmother is ill, and the doctors say there isn't anything more they can do for her. She needs help now, and she's going to need constant care in a few more months. She doesn't have any money and the facilities here are not very good for people without money. I'm going to bring her here to live with us."

And she did. Cherie brought her grandmother to live with them for the last few months of her life. And she loved her and honored her and grieved as life ebbed out of her and then as she finally passed away. The horrible wrong from Cherie's early years never got in the way. Cherie loved and cherished her grandmother, and her grandmother loved and cherished her. God made everything work and it became a rich time for Cherie and her family.

Jesus' words showed their truth and power for Cherie and her family ... "Again I say to you, if two of you agree on earth about anything they ask, it will be done for them by my Father in heaven." (Matthew 18:19)

The whole family found freedom through forgiving and reconciling after Cherie took the first step.

With God all things are possible.

Appendix - Helpful Resources

The following resources will be helpful in going deeper in understanding about forgiving and reconciling. The list isn't intended to be exhaustive, just helpful!

Victory Over the Darkness, by Neil T. Anderson. Dr. Anderson works through what it means to understand our spiritual position in Christ, and how to see ourselves as God sees us. There is a very valuable chapter on forgiveness.

The Bondage Breaker, by Neil T. Anderson. Dr. Anderson explains how Satan gains footholds in our lives, and how to deal with those footholds and rid ourselves of the enemy's torment using the truth of the scripture.

Caring Enough to Confront, by David Augsburger. Dr. Augsburger explains how and why to confront issues in relationships ... a skill critical in reconciling with others.

Keep Your Love On, by Danny Silk. Pastor Silk has great wisdom in putting relationships on healthy ground. The section on boundaries is invaluable.

Forgive and Forget: Healing the Hurts We Don't Deserve, by Louis Smedes. Dr. Smedes thoroughly covers the what, why and how to forgive in this classic.

www.ingramcontent.com/pod-product-compliance
Lightning Source LLC
Chambersburg PA
CBHW071411040426
42444CB00009B/2206